TAGORE AND ME

TAGORE AND ME

TAGORE AND ME

English Translation of Selected Poems of Rabindranath Tagore

Debidas Ray

PARTRIDGE
A Penguin Random House Company

To order additional copies of this book, contact
Partridge India
000 800 10062 62
orders.india@partridgepublishing.com

www.partridgepublishing.com/india

Contents

To my Late Father

ABOUT THE AUTHOR

The author, a retired Professor of Medicine and a bilingual poet of repute has recently been translating Bengali poems of Rabindranath Tagore which are regularly published in prestigious English journals in India. His background enables him to undertake these translations in rhyme and verse without deviating from the originals.

ABOUT THE BOOK

The book contains English translation of seventy five poems of Rabindranath Tagore selected by the author from Tagore's different collections as given in his book *Sanchayita*. The selected poems show the versatility of Tagore in depicting romantic and mystic aspects to the harsh reality of life and his total identity with nature from the plains of rural Bengal to the foothills of the Himalayas. These poems written over a period of five and a half decades also reflect the changes of his mood from light heartedness to the most sombre notes and evolution of his thoughts, ideas and social attitude. His amazing grasp over the feelings, psyche and behaviour of children, his sensitivity for the poor and downtrodden, his aversion to exploitation and injustice and his affirmative attitude to empowerment of women, all come out vividly through these translations and so do the passion, intricacies of thought and nuances of the original poems. These English translations written in rhyme and verse and in tandem with the cadence of the original poems avoid transcreation and any deviation from the originals. Majority of these translated poems are already published in reputed journals including the Visva-Bharati Quarterly founded by Rabindranath Tagore.

FOREWORD

Udaya Narayana Singh
RABINDRA BHAVANA, VISVA-BHARATI

A translation, like authoring original texts, is a creative act that enriches both Donor and Recipient languages. All languages that host translation go through the processes of resistance, adaptations and assimilations, and Tagore's construct, namely, Bengali language was no exception. He had himself shown the way quite early in life as to how to bring great writings from other speech communities to your own. When his turn came to render his own writing in "Other-tongue," he did not shy away from the responsibility. Tagore himself decided to take his craft to the readers of English, and did not hesitate to make necessary alterations to suit this task. The present translation has extended that activity further as Dr. Debidas Ray renders some of the chosen texts with very difficult lines into English, which had become his second mother-tongue because of long association with England and with English language.

In *'Manasi'*, Tagore asks: "Do you know of any speech that is soft, half-spoken, or one that comes out haltingly as are halted by the tears that roll by, and is pale because of one's inherent shame and fear?" (Trans: UNS) The original lines read in this manner where he poses this question, and a figurative translation follows:

> eta mṛdu, eta ādho, aśrujale bādho-bādho
> śarame sabhaye mlān eman ki bhāsā āche?

> "How soft, incomplete, indecision choked with tears
> How pale are the words tied in shame and fear?"   (Translation: UNS)

Then he answers the question himself, when he says—"Don't speak in words what has been already spoken by your eyes" (*'kathāy bolo nā tāhā ānkhi jāhā baliyāche'*), as he would like the urge that lies trapped within one's heart be let free (as in *'uriyā berāk sadā hṛdayer kātaratā'*). This is because if one spoke one's feelings in language, there is a chance that the magic of illusion will be dispelled (*'kathā diye bala jadi moha bhenge jāy pāche'*). Although it is true that spoken in another language, a Poet's words and their magic may not be as effective even though one cannot deny the power of great translations that happened in all ages, one still needs to restate or paraphrase great lines in other languages.

Debidas begins with a very difficult text (under 'Life') where Tagore says that he would love to live in each reader's and listener's mind, and would not like to die a death that would take him away from this beautiful world. If there is any possibility, he would like to weave songs for and about the common man picking up stories from their tears and laughter. This particular 14-liner sonnet was hand-picked by his erudite lawyer-friend Sir Ashotosh Chowdhury (1860-1924) to open his 1887-anthology *'Kari o Komal'*. The next text (under the theme—'Say it clearly to me!') is from his 1890-collection—*Mānasi*—an intense love-lyric that reminds us of the Radha-Krishna series of sung poetry with which Tagore was obsessed in his younger days as avid reader of Vidyapati and other medieval poets. The lines such as *"ogo, bhālo kare bale jāo/bāˉśari bājāye je kathā jānāte/se-kathā bujhāye dāo/Jadi nā balibe kichu, tabe kena ese/ mukhapāne śudhu cāo!"* are an example of the appeal of Rādhā to her beloved who wishes to hear in human speech what his divine flute "spoke" once. She says that if he did not want to say anything, why he should come again and again to her to keep looking at her face!

One of the best translations of this translator is the rendering of a very difficult poem from Kṣaṇikā which is rooted in colloquialism. The original lines began in this fashion:

nīla nabaghane āṣāṛhagagane
tila thāˉi ār nāhi re
ogo, āj torā jās ne gharer
                    bāhire.
bādaler dhārā jhare jhara-jhara,
āuśer khet jale bhara-bhara
kālī-mākhā meghe o pāre āˉdhār
            ghaniyeche dekh chāhire
ogo, āj torā jās ne gharer
                    bāhire.

An avid reader would immediately notice the difficulty of converting some concepts into English expressions, but Dr. Ray seems to have done it easily under the theme 'Monsoon month of āṣāṛha' in the following manner:

The entire sky is filled with fresh blue clouds—
       not even an inch is left.
Please do not step out of the house today.
It is pouring with incessant rain—the field growing the autumn paddy
       is filled to the brim with water,
the bank on the other side appears dark with black clouds.
Please do not go out of the house today....

The texts chosen by the translator are the ones with which he grew up, and they are taken from various anthologies arranged thematically in the 'Contents' section where values such as Sacrifice, Renunciation, Broadmindedness, Fearlessness, Worthy of devotion, Bowing down, Acceptance of duty, or similar virtues fall into one type, whereas the nature-focus texts such as on Flower and fruit, In the afternoon, Palm tree or Abode and sky, and the First Day's Sun fall into another type, related to which are utopia texts like Illusion, Dream, Sceptre of justice and Fear of Bewitchment, Song of the Journey as well as The path to your creation are equally interesting poems and songs. The intense feeling as expressed through some other poems such as *'Ajike tumi ghumāo—āmi jāgia rabo dāre'* (Alone), or *'Kahila gabhīr rātre sansāre bairāgī'* (Renunciation as mentioned earlier), or even *'Jemon āchho temni eso, ār koronā sāj'* (As you always are) make the task of translation really challenging. As admitted by the translator, he is aware of the kind of criticism faced by the previous translations by others from both Bengali and International scholars. I would, therefore, like to compliment the translator who is perhaps excellent in wielding his pen as well as his stethoscope with equal felicity. I have read his translations some of which had appeared in the Visva-Bharati Quarterly earlier but this book gives the Tagore-lovers and practitioners of translation a good text to test their wares of inter-lingual transfers. I wish the translator all success in future endeavours, because I think Dr. Debidas Ray would not rest with only this translation book alone.

Santiniketan,
15.4.2015

PREFACE

At the onset I should explain why I chose this title for my book. I was born in a semi urban town in Rabindranath Tagore's undivided Bengal. Considerable part of my childhood was spent in rural Bengal. I grew up in the same natural settings as Tagore's under the same sky, woken up by the same *Koel, Shalik* and other birds, amongst the same Bamboo, Tamarind and Palm trees, smelt the same fragrance of his *Shefali, Bakul, Parul* and *Rajanigandha* flowers, experienced the rigors and pleasantness of Bengal's six seasons and the twelve months, also witnessed the sowing and harvest of paddy, linseed and hemp etc, that he names in his poems. Nature seen through Tagore's eyes is familiar to me. I feel at home when I read what he wrote and think what he thought.

Tagore was alive when I was born; I have memory of the day he died. My childhood and school days were spent listening to stories about his poetry, his achievements and awards, reading his poems and short stories in text books, reciting Tagore's poems in competitions and taking part in group dances and singing Tagore songs. Long before it became the National Anthem, we sang all stanzas of *'Jana gana mana'*—in chorus in school. Where ever one goes in Bengal, one cannot avoid listening to his songs in public and private functions and at homes. As far as I myself and for generations that followed in Bengal—East and West—it has been Tagore all the way and now manifested in their national anthems.

In school days, I wrote Bengali poems which were published in school and local magazines and translated a few English poems into Bengali. After leaving school, I joined the premedical Intermediate Science course at the Ramakrishna Mission Vidya Mandir at Belur Math, Howrah. Beside studies, there were regular prayers and amid religious fervour and functions we were kept busy. I should also mention one thing of note that happened here. At the end of the final college examination, amongst the famous books I received as merit award, there was the 4th edition of *Sanchayita* which is in my possession till today. Actually most of the poems I translated were taken from this worn out book till I acquired the 11th edition of the same

After I joined the Medical College, Kolkata, all literary work had to take a sabbatical leave In between I wrote a few fun poems which my class mates still recite when we meet. However, in college days, I managed to attend a few important functions staging Tagore's songs, dances and dramas at Jorasanko Thakurbari, his ancestral home in Kolkata. Thereafter I spent a decade in U.K. where after completing post graduate studies, I worked in several hospitals. Only link with Tagore during this period was recorded tapes of Tagore songs and drama which we played whenever we met our close friends.

After coming back to India, I spent three years in Maulana Azad Medical College, New Delhi before I joined the Christian Medical College and Hospital, Vellore and I was very busy with my professional work. However, my writing habit never left me. I did a lot of clinical research and published scores of scientific articles in reputed National and International journals from CMC. After retirement I was selected as an Emeritus Medical Scientist by the Indian Medical Council and for the next five years carried out research projects at the ICMR Centre at Chennai. With abatement of routine work, my earlier habit of literary writing returned. I wrote Bengali poems as before and a Collection of my poems was published in year 2010. It is after the tragic death of Kalpana Chawla in the space-ship Columbia, when I was overwhelmed and started writing English poems and since then for nearly a decade I have published continuously in Poet, Poetry Today, Met-verse-Muse, Poetry World and other reputed journals in India.

It was the 150th birth anniversary of Rabindranath Tagore that prompted me to translate Tagore's poems into English which Poetry World—an international monthly—was keen on publishing and from June 2010 onwards, I published the translated poems almost every month and this continued till year 2013 which happens to be the hundredth year of his Nobel award. From year 2011 till now, Visva-Bharati Quarterly is regularly publishing my English translations of Tagore's poems. Seventy five translated poems of Tagore are included in this book. Most of them are already published in journals. They are my favourite poems and as they are collected from *Sanchayita*, the translated poems are serially arranged accordingly. Barring a few; translation of Rabindrasangeet (Tagore Songs) and previously translated poems have generally been avoided. The selected poems written from his younger age to the last lap of his life—apart from the mystic and romantic side of his persona—show his concern for the oppressed people of both sexes and the pain and humiliation they suffer in their life. Most revealing are the poems on children and the vivid description of nature with all its splendours in the minutest details.

Before undertaking the translation of Tagore's poems from 2010 onwards, I was acutely conscious of the criticism the previous translations by others had faced both from the Bengali and International critics. Here, I myself being a Bengali with a childhood background like mine have naturally been an advantage. Proper translations have obviously to be done from the original Bengal poems and learning the script, the grammar, vocabulary etc may not be enough as the ambience of the original poetry, the total mystique, intricacy of thought and the inner passion need to come through the translations. Also, to maintain a semblance of the cadence and rhyme of original poems, one needs to be a bilingual poet too. I undertook to translate Tagore's poems as a sense of duty and naturally I have jealously tried to uphold the honour of his 'Poetry-Maiden' about which Tagore was so sensitive. I have faithfully stuck to translations using simple English and taking recourse to very minor transcreation where the problem became organic in nature. I did not deviate.

I am grateful to Professor Udaya Narayana Singh for writing the Foreword for my book. He is currently Professor, Rabindra Bhavana and Chair, Centre for Endangered Languages, Visva-Bharati, Santiniketan. He had been the first Pro-Vice Chancellor of Visva-Bharati and was formerly Director of Central Institute of Indian Languages (CIIL), Government of India. A major linguist, poet, creative writer and translator he was Chief of the National Translation Mission (NTR)—a project specially approved by the Prime Minister of India. I am pleased that he agreed to write the Foreword. I now, gratefully acknowledge the role of poets, editors and literary personalities who have encouraged me in this venture. Prominent among them are internationally famous poet Late Dr Krishna Srinivas and former editor of Poet, S Krishnan, Editor of Poetry World, Chennai and Pranab Kumar Majumder, Editor of Bridge-In-Making, Kolkata. I thank the editors of the Visva-Bharati Quarterly for their interest in my translations and their words of appreciation. Renowned Bengali poet, Shankha Ghosh of Kolkata always helped me when I needed any clarification of Tagore's original poems.

Coming back to family and friends, I have to make it abundantly clear that without the unstinted and dedicated support and encouragement of my wife, it would not have been possible to pursue any literary work which is time consuming and many times it meant abstaining from the lucrativeness of my professional practice. The names of Adela and Vivek who did the initial exploratory work for a digital format for a few of the translated poems should follow next. Suggestions and help on hand from K.P. Chakravarthy, Assistant Librarian, Dodd Memorial Library, Christian Medical College Vellore, towards preparation of the manuscript, has been very useful. Sri Sushyamal Kundu, a noted writer in Chennai and Dr Subodh Gopal Nandi, University Librarian, Visva-Bharati Santiniketan—recently retired—for tirelessly responding to my endless queries on clarification of poems, references from Rabindra-Rachanavali (Collections of Tagore's writings) or any other matter. I have to specially thank Dr S.G. Nandi for his earnest and sincere efforts and continuing help towards actual publication of this book at every stage and I am grateful for this. In this context, I must thank the Partridge Publishing (A Penquin Random House Company), Bloomington, USA, for publishing the book.

Lastly, if the readers of my book find my translations accurate enough and interesting that would be gratifying indeed. Additionally, through these translations, if any Bengali reader finds it easier to understand the nuances and complexities of some of the Tagore's original Bengali poems that would undoubtedly add to my satisfaction.

Debidas Ray.

VELLORE
2nd May, 2015.

CONTENTS

1. LIFE

In this beautiful world, I do not want to die,
I want to live amongst human beings.
In this sunshine, in this garden full of flowers—
Amidst thriving hearts—I wish I could find a place!
On earth, the play of life—like waves—is ever undulating,
There are partings, unions and so much laughter and tears.
By stitching songs with human joy and sorrow,
I wish I could build an immortal abode!
If I can't do that, then as long as I live,
I wish I find a place amongst you all.
So that you can pluck them in mornings and in afternoons,
I let flowers of new and newer songs to bloom.
Please collect them with a smile and then afterwards—
Throw those flowers away, if they happen to dry up.

Note:
English translation of Rabindranath Tagore's poem entitled "Pran" in his collection of poems *Kori o Komal* in *Sanchayita*, 11ᵗʰed, 2010, p.42.

The first line of the original Bengali poem—*morite chahina aami sundar bhubane*

2. SAY IT CLEARLY TO ME

Please speak and say it clearly to me.
What you tried to convey through the tune of your flute,
Please explain that to me.
If you are not going to say anything, then why come and
Just look at my face.

It is pitch-dark tonight.
The stars of the sky are totally hidden under cover of the clouds.
It is the monsoon wind that is fervently spreading everywhere,
a message of despair.

I will make my tresses loose.
I will cover you with part of my *sari* under my thick dark hair,
In a tight embrace with my arms, I will lift your downcast face,
gently onto my bosom.

There in the solitude of homely comfort,
You can go on speaking whatever you want on my tryst-contented breast.
I will keep on listening with my eyes closed without looking at your face.

When you stop speaking,
We will stay put like painted dolls, staying where we are.
Only the rustle of the creepers will whisper away at the
Head end of our bed.

At the end of the night,
When the sun appears—for a moment—we will look
at each other's face.
Then slowly we will both go home following our own paths
With eyes moistened with tears.

So, please say it clearly to me.
The message you conveyed through your eyes and your flute,
Please explain that to me.
Why simply-with a trembling voice—just mumbling you come and sing.

Note:
English translation of Rabindranath Tagore's poem entitled "Bhalo kore bole jao" from his collection of poems *Manasi* in *Sanchayita* 11th.ed, 2010 p.98.

The first line of the original Bengali poem—*ogo, bhalo kore boley jao*

3. SACRIFICE.

In my vineyard today,
the fruits have appeared in clusters.
Burdened with overbearing pain
it seems they will burst open any moment
and the strong breeze of the spring
will bring them down to the ground.
Filled with juice—in uncontrollable enthusiasm—
The fruits have grown in tiers, one upon another.

Please come to my arbour, you the saviour of mine.
Filling the expanse of your apparel,
Plunder away all that I possess in life,
In silence and in utmost humility,
That's a token of total surrender by the spring.
Come; smilingly take away every bit of this
pain-filled offering from the forest.

Damaged they are by your pearly nails,
It is better to cut down the stalks themselves.
Then happily sitting under the creepers whole day,
—as if unmindfully engaged in some casual work—
with your lazy fingers, playfully pick them up one by one.
Let the bite of your teeth between the lips,
Crush those fully ripened fruits.

In my vineyard today,
the restless bees are busy humming.
Throughout the day the unwieldy wind is blowing
with a rustling sound,
With the stir in the heart of the forest,
the new tree-leaves are fluttering away.
In my vineyard today,
The fruits have come out in multitudes.

Note:
English translation of Rabindranath Tagore's poem entitled "Utsarga" from his collection of poems *Chaitali* in *Sanchayita*, 11th ed, 2010 pp. 275-6.

The first line of the original Bengali poem—*aaji more drakkha kunjabane*

4. RENUNCIATION

In dead of night said a man who became averse to material world,
"I will leave home for the sake of my deity of worship.
Who has bewitched me and attached me here?"
God said, "It's me." But he didn't listen.
Holding the child—who was fast asleep—in a tight embrace,
his beloved too was peacefully sleeping in the bed.
"Who are you both, the deceptive symbols of attachment," he asked.
God said," It's me" It went unheeded.
Leaving aside the bed, he shouted, "Oh Lord where are you?"
God said "I am here" Still, he didn't listen.
Meanwhile, the child pulled its mother and cried in its dream.
God said "Come back" But he didn't listen to His words.
God then sighed and said to Himself,
"Alas, where is my devotee going, leaving me behind?"

Note:
English translation of Rabindranath Tagore's poem entitled "Bairagya" from his collection of poems Chaitali in Sanchayita, 11th ed.2010 p.276.

The first line of the original Bengali poem—*kahilo gabhir raatre sansare biragi.*

5. FERRY

The ferry-boat goes across the stream,
from one bank of the river to the other.
Someone happens to go home, someone comes from house.
In both villages on either side, people know one another,
There is coming and going from morning till evening.

How many conflicts, how much destruction happens on earth!
New and newer history is made—
Amidst the flow of blood, froth comes up,
How many golden crowns come and disappear!
Civilisation induces lots of new and newer thirst and hunger,
How much deadly poison, how much nectar continues to emerge!

It is only here on these two banks—quite oblivious of names-
The two villages just keep looking at each other.
This ferrying goes on forever and ever, across the stream—
Someone happens to go home, someone comes from house.

Note:

English Translation of Rabindranath Tagore's poem entitled "Kheya" from his collection of poems Chaitali in Sanchayita, 11ᵗʰ ed. 2010 p.279.

The first line of the original Bengali poem—*kheya nauka parapar kare nadisrate*

6. DIDI

The migrant labourers are digging the soil
on the river bank for arranging bricks for the kiln.
Their little daughter goes up and down the ghat and
endlessly rubs and cleanses cups, pitchers and plates.
She comes to the ghat in rapid strides many times a day
Her brass bangles strike the brass plates making a
clattering noise—very busy she is throughout the day.

Her younger brother with shaven head, mud all over body
and without any clothes follows her like a tamed bird.
As per order of didi—the elder sister—he keeps sitting still
on the high river bank showing remarkable patience.

In the end, with filled water-pot on head, with plates
held in her left armpit, the little girl then trots along
holding the child's hand with her right hand.
Representative of their mother, this tiny little didi
is overburdened with work—she really is.

Note:
English translation of Rabindranath Tagore's poem entitled "Didi" in his collection of poems *Chaitali* in *Sanchayita*, 4th.ed, 1943, p281.

The first line of the original Bengali poem—*nadi tire maati kate saajaite panja*

Published in POETRY WORLD, vol. 3(no10), February2011, pp33-34.

7. INTRODUCTION

One day I came across a naked boy on the bank of the river
He was sitting happily on the ground with outstretched legs.
Down the steps of the ghat, in the water, his elder sister
was picking up lumps of mud, putting it round the jug
and then polishing and cleaning the metal-pot thoroughly.

A kid goat with soft hairs was grazing around on the bank
Suddenly it came up and stopped in front of the boy,
It looked at his face and kept on bleating intermittently.

The boy got startled and out of fright started crying loudly.
His sister at once left the pot behind and rushed to the bank
She promptly picked up the boy on one side of her lap
                                    and the goat on the other
She caressed them and comforted them in equal measure.
With animal kid on one side and the human kid on the other,
the sister gently introduced the two, to a bond of friendship.

Note : .
English translation of Rabindranath Tagore's poem entitled 'Parichay' in his collection of poems *Chaitali* in *Sanchayita*, 4th.ed, 1943, p282

The first line of the original Bengali poem—*ekdin dekhilam ulanga se chhele*

Published in POETRY WORLD, vol.3(no 10), February 2011, pp34-35

8. COMPANION

I just remember an incident of another day.
One afternoon at the side of an open field
A gypsy girl sitting on a patch of green grass
was tressing her hair into a plait all on her own.
A pet puppy coming from behind saw her moving hair,
Mistaking it for just a plaything,
the puppy—making loud noise—kept jumping
and biting the plait again and again.
The girl disapproved by shaking her head,
But this only encouraged the puppy further.
She then hit it with her finger,
Thinking that was a play, the puppy became more enthused.
The girl then laughed, hugged it to her chest
and caressed it with fondness and affection.

Note:

English translation of Rabindranath Tagore's poem entitled "Sangi" in his collection of poems *Chaitali* in *Sanchayita* 4th.ed, 1943, p283.

The first line of the original Bengali poem—*aarek diner katha pore gelo mone*

Published in POETRY WORLD, vol.3 (no9), January 2011, p29.

9. DIRECT PRACTICE

The wasp commented, "Such a tiny honey comb,
and the bee is so boastful just for this!"
The bee replied, "Brother, you come forward
and make one even smaller for us to see."

Note:

English translation of Rabindranath Tagore's poem entitled "Haate-kalame"
in his collection of poems *Kanik*ain *Sanchayita*, 4th ed, 1943, p289

The first line of the original Bengali poem—*bolta kahilo a jay khudro monchak*

Published in POETRY WORLD, vol 3 (no7), November2010, pp19-20.

10. FAMILY DISCORD

Mango said, "Oh Brother Maakaal,*
Once upon a time, we all lived in the forest as equals.
When human beings came, they brought their taste with them—
The values began to change and the balance was lost."

Note:
Maakal: a lovely looking fruit with offensive-smelling inedible pulp.

English translation of Rabindranath Tagore's poem entitled "Griha Ved" in his collection of poems *Kanika* in *Sanchayita*, 4th ed.1943, p289

The first line of the original Bengali poem—*aamro kahe, ekdin hey makal bhai*

Published in POETRY WORLD, vol. 4(no 11) March 2012, p60.

11. RELATIONSHIP OUT OF NECESSITY

A beggar's cloth-bag said to a money-bag,
"Have you forgotten that we are relatives?"
The money-bag said, "If what I possess
                    had gone to your bag,
you too would have forgotten me."

Note:
English Translation of Rabindranath Tagore's poem entitled "Garajer Atmiyata" in his collection of poems *Kanika* in *Sanchayita*, 4th ed, 1943.p289

The first line of the original Bengali poem—*kahilo bhikkar jhuli takaar thalire*

Published in POETRY WORLD vol 4(no2), June, 2011 p27

12. KINSHIP

The kerosene flame warned the earthen lamp,
"If you dare to call me brother I will throttle you."
Kerosene flame instantly exclaimed,
"Welcome—Dada—my elder brother."

Note:

English translation of Rabindranath Tagore's poem entitled "Kutumbita" in his collection of poems *Kanika* in *Sanchayita,* 4thed. 1943, p28

The first line of the original Bengali poem *kerosin shikha baley matir pradipe*

Published in POETRY WORLD, vol 3 (no5), September 2010, p52.

13. BROAD MINDED

In the hole of the wall has blossomed a tiny
and very humble flower which has no family,
                    which has no name
Others in the forest condemned it shouting,
                    "Shame, Shame"
When the sun rose it said to the flower
"Are you alright brother?"

Note:

English translation of Rabindranath Tagore's poem entitled "Udaaracharitanam" in his collection of poems *Kanika in Sanchayita*, 4th ed, 1943, p290

The first line of the original Bengali poem—*prachirer chhidre ek namgotrahin*

Published in POETRY WORLD, vol4 (no11), March 2012, p59.

14. DIRECT PROOF

Thunder says, "As long as I stay far away,
My sound is taken as that of the cloud.
My radiance too is taken as radiance
                              of the lightening.
Only when it strikes someone's head,
It is said—that's Thunder no doubt."

Note:

English translation of Rabindranath Tagore's poem entitled "Pratakshya Praman" from his collection of poems *Kanika* in *Sanchayita*, 4th ed.1943, p290.

Original Bengali poem first line—*bajra kahe dure aami thaki jatakhan*

Published in POETRY WORLD, vol4(no 11), March 2012, p59-60.

15. WORTHY OF DEVOTION

It is chariot festival; crowds are thronging the streets,
There is great pomp and grandeur on show—
The devotees lie prostrate on road and pay their obeisance.
The road felt it must be the God they were praying to,
The chariot harboured similar thoughts,
The idol too considered itself to be the deity concerned,
While the Omnipotent Almighty had a good laugh.

Note:

English translation of Rabindranath Tagore's poem entitled "Bhakti Bhajan" in his collection of poems *Kanika* in *Sanchayita*, 4ᵗʰ.ed. 1943, p290.

The first line of the original Bengali poem—*rathajatra lokaranya maha dhumdham*

Published in POETRY WORLD, vol 3(no7), November 2010, p19.

16. BOWING DOWN

The rise of the sun will erode its glory.
Still the early morning moon says with
a calm face,
"I am waiting in the shore of the sea
whilst setting,
I shall pay obeisance to the rising sun
before I depart."

Note:

English translation of Rabindranath Tagore's poem entitled "Noti Swikar" in his collection of poems *Kanika* in *Sanchayita*, 4th ed, 1943, p291

The first line of the original Bengali poem—*tapan udaye hobe mahimar khay*

Published in POETRY WORLD, vol.4(no11), March2012, p59.

17. ACCEPTANCE OF DUTY

Who will take over my duty?"
Shouted the setting Sun.
World listened, didn't respond
Like a picture, silent it stood.
An earthen lamp which was present
However, promptly proclaimed,
"My Lord, whatever little I can do,
I will do it with all my might."

Note:

English translation of Rabindranath Tagore's poem entitled "Kartabya Grahan" in his collection of poems *Kanika* in *Sanchayita*, 4th.ed. 1943, p291.

The first line of the original Bengali poem—*ke loibey mor karija kahe sandharobi.*

Published in POETRY WORLD, Vol.3 (No2), JUNE 2010, p32..

18. ILLUSION

The bank of the river on this side breathes out and says,
"I believe all that is happiness is there on the other side."
The bank of the river on the other side heaves a sigh
and laments, "Whatever happiness there can be,
must all be there on the opposite side."

Note

English translation of Rabindranath Tagore's poem entitled "Moha" in his collection of poems *Kanika in Sanchayita,* 4th ed.1943, p292

The first line of the original Bengali poem—*nadir apar kahe chhariya niswas*

Published in POETRY WORLD, vol.4(no11), March, 2012, p60

19. FLOWER AND FRUIT

Flower shouted, "Fruit, oh Fruit,
how far away are you from me?"
Fruit replied, "Sir, why do you shout,
I always reside right inside you."

Note:

English translation of Rabindranath Tagore's poem entitled "Phool O Phal" in his collection of poems *Kanika* in *Sanchayita*, 4th ed.1943, p292

The first line of the original Bengali poem—*phool kahe phukaria phal ore phal*

Published in POETRY WORLD, vol 3(no5), September 2010, p53.

20. BEYOND QUESTION

Oh ocean, over the ages what has been the
language of your own ?
The ocean replied, "The never ending inquiry
of mine."
What's the reason behind your stillness,
Oh King of mountains?
"It is my eternal silence", replied the Himalayas.

Note:

English Translation of Rabindranath Tagore's poem entitled 'Prasner Ateet" in his collection of poems *Kanika* in *Sanchayita* 4th ed.1943.p292.

First line of the original Bengali poem—*hey samudra, chirakal ki tomar bhasa*

Published in POETRY WORLD, vol 4(no2), June 2011, p.27.

21. FEAR OF BEWITCHMENT

The budding flower opened its eye
and beheld this earth—green, beautiful,
pleasant and full of musical sounds.
Just then, calling the world at large
it said, "My dear, as long as I stay,
you please stay here too."

Note

English Translation of Rabindranath Tagore's poem entitled "Moher Ashanka" in his collection of poems *Kanika* in *Sanchayita*, 4th ed, 1943. p29

The first line of the original Bengali poem—*puspa shishu ankhi meli herilo a dhara*

Published in POETRY WORLD, vol 4(no3), July 2011, pp. 18-19.

22. THE DRIVER

I happened to ask the Destiny,
"Who is it—by unrelenting brute force
is always pushing me from behind?"
Destiny replied, "Turn around and see."
When I paused, I found out that
it was my own self that I left behind
who was pushing me to the front.

Note:

English translation of Rabindranath Tagore's poem entitled "Chaalak" in his collection of poems *Kanika* in *Sanchayita*, 4ᵗʰed, 1943, p293.

The first line of the original Bengali poem—*adristire shudhalem chiradin pichche*

Published in POETRY WORLD, vol 3 (no7), November 2010, p19.

23. SAME ENDING

Sefali told the star, "I have been shed."
The star said, "My work is finished too—
We went on to fill the night's parting tray,
we the star of the sky and *Sefali* of forest."

Note

Sefali: Horshinghar, a white fragrant autumnal flower English Translation of Rabindranath Tagore's poem entitled "Ek Parinam" in his collection of poems *Kanika* in *Sanchayita*, 4th ed, 1943.p293

The first line of the original Bengali poem—*shefali kahlio aami jharilaam tara*

Published in Poetry World, vol 4 (no3), July 2011, p18.

24. DREAM

Far far away
In the dreamland of the city of Ujjaini,
One day, I went to the bank of river Shipra
to search for my first beloved
from the life of my previous birth.
Her face was made up with *lodhra* powder
and she playfully held a lotus in her hand.
She had jasmine bud in root of her ears
and *kurubak* flower on her hair.
She wore a red cloth on her slim body
which was tied at her waist,
her anklets tinkled gently on her feet.
On that day of spring—identifying the landmarks left behind—
I went back a long distance.

At that time, in the temple of Mahakal
the resounding sound of music of the evening *aarati* was heard.
The market place by now was empty and high up
on top of the dark buildings, the last rays of twilight were visible.
The home of my beloved
had to be reached by way of a narrow tortuous path,
it was hard to access and was in a solitary place.
A conch-shell and a discus were painted on the door.
By the sides of the door two young *kadamba* trees were
being nurtured like children with loving care.
The white pillar of the main gate was decorated
with the imposing figure of a lion sitting proudly.

The pigeons of my beloved had come back home and
the peacock was fast asleep on top of the golden rod.
Just at that moment, with a lamp in her hand
slowly came down my Malabika.
She appeared on the step near the door
like Lakshmi of the evening holding the evening star in hand.

The fragrance of the flowers from her body
and the smell of incense from her hair
exhaled restless air all over me.
Through her loosely draped apparel, the partially covered
left breast decorated with sandal paste was visible.
She stood like an idol in the quietness of the evening
when the din of the city had subsided by then

Slowly she put down the lamp at the door
and then came in front of me.
Putting her hand on mine
she quietly asked with sad eyes,
"Are you alright my friend?"
When I looked at her, I tried to speak but couldn't.
I had forgotten the relevant words.
We both tried hard to recollect our names but failed.
We looked at each other and kept thinking
while tears ceaselessly rolled down through
our staring eyes.

How we just kept pondering under the tree by the door.
Didn't realize when and under what pretext
her delicate hand had crept into my right hand
seeking shelter like a bird in the evening.
Her face—like a lotus with a broken stem—
slowly descended on my chest.
Anxious and forsaken—her breath
quietly mingled with mine.

The darkness of night obliterated the city of Ujjaini.
Not aware, when the lamp at the door
had got blown off by the strong wind
and at the bank of the river Shipra
the *aarati* at the Siva temple came to a halt.

Note:

lodhra: a cosmetic powder from the bark of Lodhra tree
*kurubak :*a red flower.
aarati: greeting a deity by waving a lamp.
Kadamba:The Nauclea kadamba—a tropical tree with flowers.

English translation of Rabindranath Tagore's poem entitled "Swapna" in his collection of poems *Kalpana* in *Sanchayita,* 11th ed.2010, pp.300-302

The first line of the original Bengali poem—*dure bahudure/Sapnaloke ujjainipure*

Published in POETRY WORLD, vol5.(no3), July 2012, pp31-33

25. PASSENGER

Yes, there is place.
You are on your own just carrying
a bundle of paddy.
There may be a bit more crowding
but not much–
may be my boat will be little heavier
but why should you go away for that?
Yes, there is place.

Come; please come on to the boat.
If there is dust on your feet, let it be.
Your body is as slender as a creeper,
there is restlessness in corner of your eyes—
the apparel you are wearing has the
colour of pale blue cloud.
For you, there will be a place.
Come; please come onto the boat.

Passengers are many.
They will disembark in different ghats, no one
knows the other.
You too, only for a little while will be sitting
on my boat,
when your journey ends, even if I say no,
still you will go.
So if you have come, you too are welcome.
Passengers are many.

Where do you stay?
Which barn would you deposit this bundle
of paddy?
If you don't want to say, then what do I gain
if I insist.
When I end my ferry, I will just sit and wonder–
which locality will you go, where do you stay?

Note:

English Translation of Rabindranath Tagore's poem entitled "Yatri" in his collection of poems *Khanika* in *Sanchayita*, 4ᵗʰ ed.1943 p417.

The first line of the original Bengali poem—*aachhe, aachhe sthan*

Published in POETRY WORLD, vol4 (no7), November 2011, pp20-21.

26. IN SAME VILLAGE

We both stay in the same village,
that's the only happiness we have for share.
When Bengal Robin sings in their tree—
it brings flutter to my chest, right here.
The two sheep she keeps,
they graze around under our banyan tree,
I pick them on my lap
if they damage our fence when they break free.
The name of this village of ours is Khanjana,
the name of this river of ours is Anjana.
People at large in my village, all know my name,
the name of her of ours, as we know her, it is Ranjana.

Both our localities are very near to each other,
only a field in between separates the two.
Many honey bees from their forest
make honeycomb here in our forest too.
Garlands of *Jaba*—offered for puja—from their ghat
drift onto the concrete ghat of ours,
the basket of *Kusum* flowers from their place
comes for sale, in our open market here.
The name of this village of ours is Khanjana,
the name of this river of ours is Anjana.
People at large in my village, all know my name,
the name of her of ours, as we know her, it is Ranjana.

The mango forest gets filled with blossom
in the lanes of this village of ours.
When linseed appears in their field,
hemp blooms in plants in our fields here.
When stars appear on their roof-top,
southern breeze blows on my roof-top at the time.
When monsoon rains pour in her forest,
the *Kadamba* flowers bloom in this forest of mine.

The name of this village of ours is Khanjana,
the name of this river of ours is Anjana.
People at large in my village, all know my name,
the name of her of ours, as we know her, it is Ranjana

Note:
Jaba: a red species of China rose. *Kusum*: a fragrant flower
*Kadamba: The Nauclea kadamba::*a tropical flower.
English translation of Rabindranath Tagore's poem entitled "Ak Gnaye" in his collection of poems *Khanika* in *Sanchayita*, 4th ed, 1943, pp418-19.

The first line of the original Bengali poem—*aamra dujan ekti gnaey thaki*

Published in POETRY WORLD, vol4(no5), September 2011, pp30-31.

27. THE MONSOON MONTH OF AASAARH

The entire *aasaarh*-sky is filled with fresh blue clouds
not even an inch is left.
Please do not step out of the house today.
It is pouring with incessant rain—the field growing the autumn paddy
is filled to the brim with water,
the bank on the other side appears dark with black clouds.
Please do not go out of the house today.

The cows are repeatedly lowing—bring Dhabali to the cowshed now.
As soon as the day draws to a close, it will be dark at once.
Please stand at the door and see whether those who went
to the field have returned.
I have no idea where the cowboy spent the whole day.
As soon as the day comes to an end, it will become dark.

Listen, someone wanting to cross the river is shouting for the boatman.
Ferrying has stopped today.
The eastern wind is blowing; there is no one near the river
The waves are rolling over both the banks.
Continuous rain falling rapidly over water is making
a rippling noise.
Ferrying has stopped for the day.
Please stay indoors, do not go out of the house today.

The sky is dark, not much of the day is left.
The cloth covering her body will be soaked by the pouring rain.
The steps to the *ghat* are slippery now,
Look, how the reeds of thin bamboos are swinging wildly
by the side of the path.
Please do not go out of the house today.

Note:

English translation of Rabindranath Tagore's poem entitled "Aasaarh" in his collection of poems *Khanika* in *Sanchayita,* 11th ed.2010, p421.

The first line of the original Bengali poem—*nil nabaghane aasaarh gagane*

Published in The Visva-Bharati Quarterly Volume—22 Numbers 3& 4 October-2013—March—2014.pl.

28. AS YOU ALWAYS ARE

Come dressed as you are no need to put any more make-up.
Unkempt may be your tresses, the parting of hair may not be straight,
It doesn't matter if decoration with sandal paste is not complete.
If your bodice remains loose there is no need to feel shy.
Come dressed as you are no need to put any more make-up.

If the red colour of lac on your feet gets rubbed off—don't be afraid,
If your anklets drop off, maybe you can leave them behind.
If the pearl from your necklace comes off—have no regret.
Come hurriedly putting your feet on the grass underneath.
Look it's getting dark, the sky is covered with clouds.

On the other side, flocks of herons are flying away in rows,
In the empty field—now and then—a strong wind blows.
There, the cows of the village are rushing back to their shed.
Look it is getting dark, the sky is covered with clouds.

The lamp will just get blown off, so why simply light it,
Looking at your eyes, who can see if *kaajal* is there or not?
Your wanton and moist eyes look darker than the clouds.
Let your eyelids stay as they are, they look better that way.
Just to put *kaajal* in your eyes, why simply light the lamp?

If the garland is not stitched—my dear—there is no harm
If your make-up is not finished yet, more ornaments won't help.
The eastern sky is overcast with clouds; the day is almost gone
Come, smiling in a simple dress, no need of ornament or makeup.

Note:

kaajal: collyrium.

English translation of Rabindranath Tagore's poem entitled "Chirayamaana" from his collection of poems *Khanika* in *Sanchayita*, 11th.ed 2010, p427

The first line of the original Bengal poem—*Jemon achho temni eso, aar korona saaj*

29. IN THE AFTERNOON

In the morning, when the conch was blown in your courtyard,
Filling their flower-trays, men and women left home
and started walking along the cool forest path,
laden with fresh dew and resounding with humming noise.
Unmindfully—under the shadow of a dense leafy grove—
I was lying down on the grassy bank of a river
amidst warble of the birds and a gentle breeze.

Oh Lord, I did not go for your *puja*—
I didn't even see who the people were walking along the path.
Today I feel that it was better that I erred,
At that time of the day, the flowers were buds only.

One can see them blooming throughout the day.
I have filled this puja-tray of mine, in the afternoon only.

Note:
puja: hindu prayers.
English translation of Rabindranath Tagore's poem entitled "Aparanhe" in his collection of poems *Naibedya* in *Sanchayita*, 11th ed, 2010, p.438.
The first line of the original Bengali poem-*prabhate jakhan sankha utechhilo baaji*

30. SCEPTRE OF JUSTICE

Your sceptre of Justice—you yourself
have handed over to everyone's hand
and to each one of us—Oh Emperor-
you have given the responsibility to rule.
This great honour, this onerous task—
I hope I am able to accept humbly
to bear on my head with reverence,
I should be able to discharge the duty
you assigned, without fearing anyone.

Where pardon means feeble weakness,
Oh ferocious Lord—as per your diktat-
I should be able to be ruthless in such cases.
The stark truth—at your instance—should
blurt out of my tongue like a sharp sword.
By taking my place in your seat of Judgment
I should be able to uphold your honour.

The one who commits injustice and the one
                         who tolerates the same
Let your hatred burn them alike like a bundle of straw.

Note:
English translation of Rabindranath Tagore's poem entitled 'Nyay Dando'
from his collection of poems *Naibedya in Sanchayita* 4[th]ed, 1943.p441-442

The first line of the original Bengali poem—*tomar nayer dando protyeka kare*
Published in The Visva-Bharati Quarterly Volumes:19-20, October-2010-
September—2011, p.110.

31. ABODE AND SKY

You yourself are the sky, yourself the abode—
you are one and the same.
Oh beautiful you, in your earthly abode
love runs deep.
At each moment, in many colours
in many aroma and music,
the enchanted life has enclosed it
from all sides.
Here, the dawn, holding a golden plate
in right hand,
brings a garland that is elegant
to place it silently over the forehead of earth.
With its face down the evening comes
in open fields after the cows have gone
and by treading the unbeaten path brings in
the golden pitcher after filling it with sacred water
from the western seas.

Wherever you happen to be the sky of our soul
—the boundless area of transition—
what prevails there is incandescent glow.
There exists no day, no night, not a single
person or creature,
There is no trace of colour or smell,
let alone any voice.

Note:
English translation of Rabindranath Tagore's poem entitled "Neerh O Aakash"
in his collection of poems *Naivedya* in *Sanchayita*, 11ᵗʰ ed.2010, p443

The first line of the original Bengali poem—*ekaadhare tumi aakash tumi neerh*

Published in POETRY WORLD, vol.5(no7), November 2012, pp28-29.

32. BIRTH

At what point of time,
I entered through the portal of life
to the abode of this wonderful world,
that particular moment was not known to me.
I did not know what was the power that
-like the buds in a large forest at dead of night-
made me blossom on the lap of this great mystery.

Yet in the morning, holding the head high,
the moment I opened my eyes and surveyed this world,
dressed in a sky-blue apparel stringed with golden rays
and came across this earthly life
—embedded with joy and sorrow—
then at once, it seemed to me that
like my mother's bosom this unknown mystery
was extremely familiar and exclusively mine.

Apparently, shapeless and beyond comprehension-
that awesome power has assumed the shape
of my mother and appeared in front of me.

Note:

English translation of Rabindranath Tagore's poem entitled "Janma" in his collection of poems *naivedya* in *Sanchayita*, 11th ed. 2010, pp443-444

The first line of the original Bengali poem—*jibaner singhadare pashinu jey khane*
Published in POETRY WORLD, vol.6 (no.3), July 2013, p59.

33. ALONE

Today you sleep—I will keep vigil at the door
and keep the lamp burning
On your part you have loved me, today it's me alone
who have to love you.
You don't have to dress up for me any more—
from now on for you
I will keep my heart decorated with flowers
throughout day and night.

Your hands for so long, ignoring any fatigue
have gone on serving me,
Today after withdrawing them from all work
I will bear them on my head.
After finishing your acts of devotion now you are going away
surrendering heart and soul,
From this time onwards you accept my worship with tears
and my songs of praise.

Note:
English translation of Rabindranath Tagore's poem entitled 'Ekaki' from his collection of poems *Smaran* in *Sanchayita* 4thed, 1943.pp 448-449

The first line of the original Bengali poem—*aajike tumi ghumao—aami jagia robo dare*

Published in Poetry World, vol. 6(no4), August 2013, p50.

34. HIDE AND SEEK

If I play a mischievous trick and blossom as a flower
in the *Chanpa* tree
and early in the morning roll over the tender leaves
of the branch,
you would then—Oh Mother—loose out to me
as it is doubtful that you would be able to recognise me.
You will be shouting "Khoka, where are you?"
I will just keep quiet and smile.

When you will be busy doing your chores,
I will keep a watch over it all with my eyes open.
After taking bath—with your hair unkempt—
you will pass the *Chanpa* tree as you go to the
puja room from where you will be getting smell
of the flowers coming from a distance.
At the time, you will not know that the smell
that was coming was from your Khoka's body.

In the afternoon after others have finished their meal,
you will sit down with the *Mahabharata* in your hand
and the shadow of the tree coming through the window
will fall on your back and on your lap.
On my part, I will be swinging my tiny shadow
over the pages of your book.
Even then, you won't have any idea that it is the
shadow of your Khoka that is floating across your eyes.

In the evening after lighting the lamp
you will proceed to the cow-shed
and at that time, mother—acting like a flower—
I will shed myself and drop to the ground.
Again I will become your Khoka and will come to you
and demand, "Please tell me a story."
You will ask, "You naughty boy, where have you been?"
I will simply say, "That I won't tell you."

Note:

Chanpa: a flower of Magnolia family

Mahabharata: the greatest epic of India.

English translation of Rabindranath Tagore's poem entitled "Lukochuri" in his collection of poems *Shishu* in *Sanchayita*, 11th ed. 2010, pp452-453.

The first line of the original Bengali poem—*aaami jodi dustumi kore*

Published in POETRY WORLD, vol.5(no6), October 2012, pp31-32.

35. DECEPTION

Lest I understand you easily,
Is it that, why you are so playful?
When you burst out into laughter
You may have tears locked inside.
I follow your deceptive ways fully,
The things you want to say
You never ever come out with.

Lest, I catch up with you easily
May be that's why you are wayward.
In case I treat you at par with others,
You became hostile and awkward.
I understand your deceptive ways clearly
The path you want to follow
You never walk that way.

Because you want more than others
Is it that why you leave the scene?
Casually and with contempt
You toss aside the gift package.
I can now see through you thoroughly,
What is satisfactory for others
Never satisfies you.

Note:

English Translation of Rabindranath Tagore's poem 'Chhalana' in his collection of poems *Utsarga* in *Sanchayita* 4th.ed, 1943.p462

The first line of the original Bengali poem—*tomare pacchhe sahaje bujhi*

Published in The Visva-Bharati Quarterly Volumes:19-20 October-2010-September-2011, p.109.

36. FAMILIAR

How can you hide what's in your mind
When your heart emits it through your eyes
every now and then.
Today you have come in an amusing dress,
wearing a pearl-necklace and with unkempt hair
Playfully smiling through the corners of your eyes,
You came to the shoal of my heart.
I am not taken in by your oblique glance
Nor am I affected by your caustic jokes.
That you struck me with your delicate hand,
Would it make me shed tears?
Not such a fool I am.
You may well laugh at me,
I will bear it with a smile.

Today you have put on this appearance,
Hoping that would charm me.
But can you deny that you came before
to stroke my fevered brow, with your cool fingers?
I saw your speechless face
and your eyes hazy with tears
I saw your scared look and your
sad and frail figure.
In your sorrowful and steadfast eyes
I noticed sweet entreaty.
Today by trying to enforce discipline
under cover of a false smile,
If you are hoping that will scare me—
Then not such a fool I am.
You may well laugh at me,
I will bear it with a smile.

Note:

English translation of Rabindranath Tagore's poem entitled "Chena" in his collection of poems *Utsarga* in *Sanchayita*, 11th.ed.2010, pp462-63.

The first line of the original Bengali poem—*aapanare tumi koribe gopan ki kori*

37. MIRAGE

Frenzied by my own smell,
I roam through the forest
like a musk-deer.
On a *phalgun*—night in southern breeze—
I can't find my way.
What I want was wished mistakenly,
what I get I don't want.

Getting out of my chest,
my inner desire
eludes like a mirage does.
When I try to embrace it with open arms,
I can't get it back on to my chest.
What I want was wished mistakenly,
what I get I don't want.

My flute seems to prefer
to hold on to its songs
like a restless madman.
For the one that I manage to retain—
I can't find the tune.
What I want was wished mistakenly,
what I get I don't want.

Note:
phalgun :Bengali month of spring
English translation of Rabindranath Tagore's poem entitled Marichika in his
collection of poems *Utsarga* in *Sanchayita*, 11th ed. 2010, p463

The first line of the original Bengali poem—
paagal hoiya bane bane firi aaparno gandhe momo

Published in POETRY WORLD, vol 6 (no 4), August 2013, pp.52-53

38. GRACE

"Alas, who else other than the sky
can accommodate you!
Oh Sun, I only dream of you,
I am not able to serve you."
The dew lamented saying,
"That I will tie you down—Oh Sun—
I don't have such strength.
That's why, without you, my short life
is nothing but a drop of tear."

"With vast sunshine I light up the whole world,
still, I can surrender to the drop of dew
and give it my love too."
Then coming onto the bosom of the dew,
the Sun smiled to say—
"I will become smaller in size and fill you up to the full,
I will shape your short life in such a way
that it transforms into a smile."

Note:

English translation of Rabindranath Tagore's poem entitled "Prasad" in his collection of poems *Utsarga* in *Sanchayita*, 11th d 2010, p464-5

The first line of the original Bengali poem—*hai gagan nohile tomare dharibe keba*
Published in POETRY WORLD, vol.5(no 10), February 2013 pp59-60.

39. ROTATION

The incense wants to mingle with its scent,
Scent wants to cling on to the incense.
The melody wants to surrender to the verse,
Verse itself wants to rush back to melody.
Idea wants to manifest itself in shape
while shape wants to be set free in idea.
Limitless wants close company of the limit,
Limit wants to get lost in what is limitless.
Between destruction and creation—no one knows—
who agreed to this non-stop coming and going
                                    between idea and shape—
The one who is attached is searching for own freedom
while freedom wants to reside in midst of attachment.

Note:

English translation of Rabindranath Tagore's poem entitled "Aabartan" in his collection of poems *Utsarga* in *Sanchayita*, 11th ed, 2010, pp467-8

The first line of the original Bengali poem—*dhup aapanare milaitey chahe gandhey*

Published in Poetry World, vol 5 (no9) January 2013, p39.

40. PAST

Speak, you speak
Oh self-born past, in the endless night
Why do you just sit and stare?
Speak, please speak.

Era and ages come and pour their stories
into the ocean of yours
So many streams of so many lives come and mingle
with your water.
By the time they arrive they have lost their flow,
their repetitive warbles have come to a stop—
Current less and speechless—where do you take
them away?
Oh past, you speak, please speak to my heart.

Speak, please speak.
You stupefied past, the secretive you,
you are not unconscious—
Why don't you speak?
I have heard the sound of your transit
right inside my heart.
So many savings of so many days
you left behind in my soul.
Oh past, in all corners of the earth,
you keep on working secretly behind the scene.
In the fickleness of the garrulous days,
you manage to stay still.
Oh past, you speak, please speak right into my heart.

Speak, please speak.
You never happen to miss a single tale;
you pick up all of them—
So speak, please speak
In each page of life with an invisible script,

you wrote chronicles of our forefathers, delving into the core.
Those whose stories might have been forgotten by all,
you never forgot even their minutest details.
Struck dumb with amazement, all those forgotten stories
you continue to carry.
Please give them voice—oh saintly past—
Speak, please speak.

Note

English translation of Rabindranath Tagore's poem entitled "Ateet" in his collection of poems *Utsarga* in *Sanchayita*, 11th ed.2010, pp 468-69.

The first line of the original Bengali poem—*katha kau katha kau*

41. AUSPICIOUS MOMENT

Oh Mother, the Royal Prince will pass across the path
in front of my house today—
On this morning, how am I to keep myself engaged
in simply doing house chores
Tell me, how I shall dress myself,
What hair-do will be suitable for the day,
What should be the style and what colour shall I wear.
Mother, what's the matter with you,
Why are you giving me such a surprised look?
At the window-corner where I will stand,
I know, he won't even look there.
Within a moment, his visit will end
and he will go far away.
Only, the sad tune from the flute of his party will be coming
from some distant field.
Still, it is the Royal Prince who will pass across the path
in front of my house,
How can I help not dressing myself suitably for the moment?

Oh Mother, the Royal Prince just went across the path
in front of my house
The morning sun shone on the golden-peak chariot of his.
Removing my veil—from the window—
Just for a moment, I managed to see him, Mother—
I ripped apart my gem-necklace
and threw it on the dusty path.
Oh Mother, what's the matter with you,
Why are you giving me such a surprised look?
From my torn necklace, he did not pick up the gems
It got smashed under the wheels of his chariot

No one knew what I gave and to whom,
It remained hidden under the dust.
Still it is the Royal Prince who passed across the path
in front of my house
How can I help not giving away the most precious
treasure of my heart?

Note

English translation of Rabindranath Tagore's poem entitled "Subhakshman"
in his collection of poems *Kheya* in *Sanchayita*, 11th ed.2010, p487.

The first line of the original Bengali poem—*ogo maa, rajaar dulal jaabe aaji mor*

42. BY THE SIDE OF THE DRAW-WELL

I didn't want anything from you; didn't tell my name
When you said good-bye I just kept silent.

I was alone near the well, under the shade of the neem tree
The neighbours have filled their pitchers and gone away
While going, they shouted, 'Come on, the day is passing by'
I don't know what thought I had in mind, why I sat idly by.

I did not hear your footsteps or know when you came
Looking sad, in a tired voice you said you were a thirsty passer-by
Hearing you, I got startled and kept pouring water on your palms.
Leaves were rustling; cuckoo was calling at the time
The scent from the *bablah* flowers was coming
from the turning of the village-road.

When you asked me my name, I felt very shy
I wondered what I did of worth to be remembered by you.
That I could give you little water when you were thirsty,
was—itself—enough for me as a moment to treasure.

There—in the afternoons—by the side of the well,
birds still sing the same, neem leaves shake as before
and invariably, I just keep on sitting.

Note:
bablah (babul): Gum—arabic tree of India.

English translation of Rabindranath Tagore's poem entitled "Kuyar Dhare" in his collection of poems *Kheya*in *Sanchayita*, 4ᵗʰed, 1943, pp 494-95.

The first line of the original Bengali poem—*tomar kaachhe chaini kichhu janai ni mor naam*

Published in POETRY WORLD, vol 3(no11), March 2011, pp18-19.

43. DAY'S END

A dilapidated guest house,
At the cracked plinth of the house,
the peepul and banyan trees
have spread their branches.
Under the scorching sun, across the hot pathways,
somehow the day has passed.
It was in my mind that in the evening there was
a shelter available here.
Darkness descended on the fields,
those attending the open market went back to
the village.
When I arrived here and looked around,
not a single soul was present.

For a long time, many people at the end of many a day
washed off the dirt of the road and cleaned themselves
on arrival here.
In the star-studded night they sat in the
pleasantly cool courtyard
and exchanged many stories of many lands
between themselves.
At daybreak when birds sang they woke up to a new life,
Weighed down by flowers, creepers in the path
used to swing at the time.

The day I arrived here there was no lamp lit in the room,
Black marks of flame of many olden days were
depicted on the wall
On the bank of the dried up tank, fireflies hopped
around the bushes

Fallen branches of bamboo on the broken path
cast shadows of fear.
At the end of the day's journey I had no idea
whose guest I was,
Alack the long lonely night, alack the tired body
of mine!

Note:

English translation of Rabindranath Tagore's poem entitled 'Dinasesh' in his collection of poems *Kheya* in *Sanchayita*, 4ᵗʰed, 1943, p495-96

The first line of the original Bengali poem—*bhanga atithshaala*

44. DOWNTRODDEN

Oh my ill-fated land, those of yours whom you subjected to humiliation,
It's in humiliation only—you will come to be treated as equal to them.
Those of yours, whom you deprived of their basic human rights,
Kept them standing and waiting in front, never offering a seat,
It's in humiliation only—you will come to be treated as equal to them.

Keeping them away as untouchable beings, day after day,
You have denigrated the God inside the human soul.
Faced with the wrath of the Lord—sitting at the doorstep of famine—
You have to share your food and drink with all of them.
It's in humiliation only—you will come to be treated as equal to them.

Down below where you pushed them away from your exalted seat
It is right there, where you casually banished all your power.
Being trampled under the feet, it mingles with the dust—
Unless you yourself come down to the same level, there is no escape.
It's in humiliation only—you will come to be treated as equal to them.

The one whom you cast down below, he will tie you down underneath,
The one whom you are keeping behind, he will pull you from the back.
Under the darkness of ignorance, the one whom you keep out of view—
casting a shadow on your well being—he creates a deep chasm between you.
Today, it is in humiliation, you will come to be treated as equal to them.

For centuries, you are carrying the burden of that shame on your head
Even then, you never bothered to pay obeisance to the God inside men.
Yet looking down below, can you not see with your own eyes
that the God of the downtrodden and poor has descended on the dust.
It is there, in humiliation you will come to be treated as equal to them.

Can you not see that the messenger of death is standing at the door?
He is putting a mark of malediction on the arrogance of your nation.
If you don't call everyone and still prefer to stay aloof,
if you tie yourself down with strings of vanity all round—
Then in death—in the midst of the ashes of the funeral pyre—
you will be rendered equal to all.

Note:

English translation of Rabindranath Tagore's poem entitled "Apamanito" in his collection of poems *Geetanjali* in *Sanchayita,* 11ᵗʰ ed, 2010, p509.

The first line of the original Bengali poem—*hey mor durbhaaga desh jaader korechho apamaan*

Published in The Visva-Bharati Quarterly. Vol.23,
Issue No1 April 2014—June 2014 page 2

45. HIGHEST PRICE

'Who will buy me up,
who will buy everything I have?'
Shouting and declaring my wares
I roam night and day
Alas, that is the way
my day passes away—
The load on my head has become
a great burden.
Some people just come, some just laugh
and some pitifully look.

In the middle of afternoon, I was walking
on King's cobbled path,
With crown on his head, weapon in his hand,
on chariot came the King.
He got hold of my hand and said
'I will procure you by force'—
Whatever strength was there, got exhausted
in tugging and pulling.
With crown on his head, away went the King
on his golden chariot.

I was crossing through the lane
in front of a closed door.
The door opened, and out came an old man
with a purse in his hand.
He pondered and then said
'I will buy it all with gold.'
He emptied his purse and walked up and down.
Without paying attention, with load on my head,
I walked away somewhere else.

In the evening, the moon shines on a tree
full of buds.
A beautiful woman came out near the *bakul* tree.
She came near and said,
'I will buy you with my smile.'
Eventually, her smile turned into tears
and slowly she went back to the shadowed
forest land.

The sun is shining on the sea-shore,
there are waves in the sea.
A child is playing with shells on the beach.
Like someone who is familiar to me,
he said, 'I will buy you up for free'-
I was at once relieved of my load on that day.
Playfully, he bought me up without paying any price.

Note:

Bakul: an evergreen flower tree.
English translation of Rabindranath Tagore's poem entitled 'Charam Mulya' in his collection of poems *Gitimalya* in *Sanchayita,* 11th ed. 2010, pp514-515.

The first line of the original Bengali poem—*kay nibi go kine aamay/kay nibi go kine*

Published in Poetry World, vol. 6(no2), June 2013.pp58-59.

46. FATIGUE

Pardon me if I feel tired—pardon me my Lord
Pardon me if ever I lag behind on the road.
If my heart trembles like this, as it does today
Ignore that pang and pardon me Lord.

Forgive that meanness, Oh Lord,
Forgive if ever I look back.
If due to day's heat under the burning sun,
the garland offered in the puja-plate dries up
Ignore that dullness and pardon me Lord.

Note:

English translation of Rabindranath Tagore's poem entitled 'Klanti' from his collection of poems *Geetali* in *Sanchayita* 4[th]ed, 1943.p525

The first line of the original Bengali poem—*klanti aamar khama karo prabhu*

Published in The Visva-Bharati Quarterly Volume:-19-20
October-2010-September-2011 pp.109-110.

47. SONG OF THE JOURNEY

Oh you traveller, you are the friend of all fellow travellers,
It's the journey on the road that itself is an achievement of yours.
The one who sings the song of joy of journey on the road,
in his voice, it is your song that is being sung.
The one who doesn't turn around and look back,
doesn't row his boat only along the coast—
The one whose soul gets stimulus from you,
the tempest calls him to the shoreless sea.
It is the journey on the road that itself is an achievement of yours.

Oh you traveller, you are the friend of all fellow travellers,
In the heart of the passerby, it's your boat that is rowed.
The one who opens the door and looks up to the front,
it is his gaze that—in fact—keeps looking at you.
Danger or hurdles nothing does he fear,
he doesn't stay back hoping for any gain,
his mind is keen to carry on with the journey,
it is the journey for which his mind longs for—
the journey that takes him nearer to you.
It is the journey on the road that itself is an achievement of yours.

Note:
English translation of Rabindranath Tagore's poem entitled "Pather gaan" in his collection of poems *Geetali* in *Sanchayita*, 11th.ed, 2010 p527.

The first line of the original Bengali poem—*pantho tumi, pantha janer sakhaa hey*

Published in The Visva—Bharati Quarterly
Vol.23, Issue No1 April 2014—June 2014 page 1.

48. GETTING LOST

My little daughter heard a call from her
friends below and went down the stairs.
As she was afraid of the darkness
she was slow and hesitant in her steps.
She was carrying a lamp in her hand
which she covered carefully with part of her sari.

I stayed on the roof
It was spring; the month was *Chaitra*
and the night sky was full of stars.
Suddenly, I heard my daughter crying
and I hurried down to see her.
It so happened that while going down the stairs
the lamp she was carrying
had got blown off by the wind.
When I asked, "What's the matter Bami?"
She cried from below, "I have got lost.

On that starry night of *Chaitra*
when I went back to the roof top
and looked at the sky, it seemed to me
that someone like my daughter Bami
was protecting the flame of a lamp
with the expanse of her sky blue apparel
and was walking slowly all by her own.
I wondered that if by chance, the light went off
and suddenly everything came to a halt, then perhaps
she too would fill the sky with her cry and scream,
"I have got lost."

Note:

Chaitra: the last month of Bengali year (a month of spring)
English translation of Rabindranath Tagore's poem entitled "Haariye Jaaoa" in his collection of poems *Palaataka* in *Sanchayita*, 4thed. 1943, p572-573

The first line of the original Bengali poem—*chhotto aamar meye*

Published in POETRY WORLD, vol 3 (no3), July 2010, p32-33

49. TO REMEMBER

I do not remember my mother.
Only when I go out to play—at times—without any reason
Suddenly a humming tone keeps ringing in my ears,
then the memory of my mother gets mingled with my play.
May be mother used to sing while pushing away my swing—
Mother has gone but on her way she has left behind her song.

Only when in the month of *Ashwin* at the *Sefali* grove at dawn,
the smell of the flowers comes along with the dew-laden breeze,
I don't know why—the memory of mother then appears in my mind.
On certain days mother used to carry the wicker-tray with flowers—
May be the smell of the puja offerings became reminiscent of mother.

I do not remember my mother.
Only when I go and sit in the corner of the bed-room
And through the window I look at the distant sky—
then it seems that mother is looking at me with a steadfast gaze.
Holding me in her lap when mother used to look at me,
It is that look she has left behind spreading across the sky.

Note:
Ashwin: sixth month of Bengali calendar (a month of autumn)
Sefali; a white fragrant flower
English translation of Rabindranath Tagore's poem entitled 'Mone-Para' in
his collection of poems *Shishu Bholanath* in *Sanchayita* 4[th]ed, 1943, pp574-575

The first line of the original Bengali poem—*maake aamar pare na mone*

Published in POETRY WORLD, vol4(no12) April 2012, pp11-12.

50. FORGETTING TO PLAY

Do you really think that I just want to play day and night?
Listen to me mother—that's never true.
The other day when I woke up at dawn I saw
that the rains and clouds had gone
and the sun had come out coruscating through the twigs of the bamboo tree.
It was a holiday, the puja *Shehnai* was being
played in an eerie note at a distance
and three *Shaliks* were quarrelling on the thatch of the kitchen at the time.
Spreading the toys in front of me, I wondered what game to play
and that's all I thought all the time.
I didn't like any of the games and the whole day just passed away—
Holding the railings, I kept sitting in the corner of the verandah.

From time to time, there come days when I simply forget to play—
Some sort of uneasy feeling I get in my mind on that day.
It is middle of the afternoon in winter.
On someone's roof-top at a distance,
a little girl is spreading out a violet coloured *sari* in the sun to dry.
I silently keep watching and wondering if beyond there lies
that desolate and extensive field—
I imagine that must be the place where the King's palace is.
If I had a young cloud-trotting winged horse,
then tightly holding the reins, I would have at once gone there.
On my journey along the bank of the river—sitting under a tree—
I would have asked the 'tattler bird couple' the right way forward.

On certain days, I notice that you with a letter from my father in hand,
silently keep thinking something while sat leaning against the window.
Looking at your face, it seems that you are a woman from some other land
and my mother for a very long time from a far off place.

I go near just to touch your hand as if you are a mother who got lost—
A mother who is like the distant tune of a flute coming across the fields
from the base of a banyan tree.
Any thought of play drifts away as I think to myself, during what period,
in which country and on which shore of the ocean your house was?
Setting sails in a boat with you at daybreak, I wish we could go back
to that house in an unknown island.

Note:
*Shehnai;*a kind of wooden wind instrument.
*Shalik:*a tropical bird of the myna group.
English translation of Rabindranath Tagore's poem entitled "Khelabhola" in
his collection of poems *Shishu Bholanath* in *Sanchayita*, 1943, 4th ed. pp575-76.

The first line of the Original Bengali poem—*tui ki bhabis din rattir khelte aamar mon*

Published in POETRY WORLD, vol 4(no6), October 2011, pp50-51.

51. ICHCHHAMATI

If I could become whatever I wish to be whenever I want,
I would then—at once—turn myself into river Ichchhamati.
It's the bank on my right side where the sun will rise
and it is the bank on my left where the darkness
will descend in the evening.
I will speak what's in my mind to the banks on both sides—
half of it will be said during the day and the other half at night.

When I go round and round in the ghat of my own village,
just then, I keep gurgling away across the distant fields.
I know the people of this village, who come to the water to take bath,
with cows and buffalos they swim across to the other bank.
Those who come from a distance, they have dresses of a newer style—
I don't know their names, don't know their village,
it all seems so strange.

Just a ray of light sparkles across the water on top—
clapping and laughing, the fairies dance along with the waves.
Down below where the steps of the ghat have sunk,
I don't know who they all are silently staying there.
I have no idea what they are up to in the nooks and crannies,
I myself would be somewhat scared to look in that direction.

The people of the village would know only a little bit of me,
where the rest of me will get lost—I myself do not know.
On one side of the bank there will be only green everywhere
while on other side will be the scorching sun on the strip of land.
There will be comings and goings during the day,
at night there will be total silence and darkness—
just staring at the banks will give an eerie sensation over the body.

Note:

English translation of Rabindranath Tagore's poem entitled "Ichchhamati" in his collection of poems *Shishu Bholanath* in *Sanchayita*.4ᵗʰ ed, 1943.pp576-77.

The first line of the original Bengali poem—*jakhan jemon mone kari taai hote pai jodi*

Published in POETRY WORLD, vol4(no 8), December 2011, pp17-18.

52. PALM TREE

The palm tree:	Standing on one leg Rising above all other trees It peeps into the sky.
Its desire:	Piercing the dark clouds To fly away at a stroke— But where does it get wings?
That's why:	Right on top of its head Across its round leaves It spreads its wish
Thinks to itself:	May be these are the wings, Now there is no constraint in flying away leaving its abode.
Throughout the day:	Rustling and rattling Its leaves keep shaking, It feels as if it is flying-
It imagines:	Trotting in the sky Evading the stars It might go somewhere beyond.
Afterwards:	As soon as the wind weakens, The leaves stop shaking Making it think again-
When it realises:	The soil is its mother And once again it prefers its own corner on earth.

Note:

English translation of Rabindranath Tagore's poem entitled "Taal gaach" in his collection of poems *Shishu Bholanath* in *Sanchayita* 4ᵗʰ ed, 1943.pp577-578

The first line of the original Bengali poem—*taal gaachh ek paye dnariey*

Published in POETRY WORLD, vol 3(no12), April 2011, p20.

53. SUNDAY

Monday, Tuesday and Wednesday—
            they all come in such a rush,
Have they got—in their house—huge aeroplanes?
Sunday—oh mother—why it comes so late?
Slowly she arrives after all the other days
Is her house beyond the sky further away
                     than others?
Does she—oh mother—come from a poor family
                 like yours?

Monday, Tuesday and Wednesday—
they all intend to stay put,
they have no interest whatsoever
of going back home.
Who is it that hurries up Sunday so much—
the hourly bell seems to strike every half an hour.
In her house beyond the sky
her chores seem to be that much more .
Does she—oh mother—come from a poor family
                   like yours?

Monday Tuesday and Wednesday—
they all seem to have sullen faces
and apparently have great rivalry with
little children
But at the end of Saturday-night
as soon as I wake up,
what I see on Sunday's face
is a permanent smile.
When she is ready to depart
she looks at our face with tears in her eyes.
Does she—oh mother—come from a poor family
                 like yours?

Note:
English translation of Rabindranath Tagore's poem entitled "Robibar" in his collection of poems *Sishu Bholanath* in *Rabindra Rachanavali* Vol 2, p 579

The first line of the original Bengali poem—*som mangal budh era sab aase taratari*

Published in POETRY WORLD, vol. 5 (no 12), April2013, pp.35-36.

54. THE OTHER MOTHER

Instead of being mine, if you were to become someone else's mother,
you might think then I wouldn't have recognised you
nor would I have gone to your lap.
It would have been much more fun—
Our houses would have been in two different places,
I would have lived in this village and you in the village on the other bank.
Here—in this place—during the day,
I would have played whatever I could play
and at the end of the day, I would have crossed over to you by boat.
Suddenly coming from behind
I would have said, "Tell me who I am?"
You would have wondered that though I looked familiar,
you didn't know exactly who I was.
I would then jump on to your lap
and putting my arms around your neck I would say,
"You have to recognise me—I am your Abu only."

When you would come to collect water on the other bank,
guess who would come to the ghat on this side at the time.
Making a boat out of paper,
I would float it towards you.
Even if it reached you, would you have known whose boat it was?
I did not learn how to swim,
otherwise, I myself would have gone
and swum across from this side to the bank of yours.
Between mother's bank and that of Abu
a gap would have remained—
One could not touch the other—both staying separately.
Roaming around during the day,
seeing each other from a distance,
when evening came, Abu and his mother would be united again.

But suppose suddenly someday Bipin, the boatman
            had refused to take me to your side mother,
      By that time, lighting the lamp in the house
            and spreading the mat across on the roof-top,
you would have sat down with old Khantaburi sitting near your feet.
      The group of seven stars would have appeared in the sky,
            the fox would howl in the paddy-field
and like a fleeting shadow, the bat would flit away somewhere else.
Seeing the delay in my coming, wont you then be getting scary spells—
Thereafter, mother, you would surely cross over and come to Abu's side.
            Would I in that case let you escape,
            Would I ever let you go back again—
The bank of mother on the other side then had to surrender to Abu's bank.

Note:
English translation of Rabindranath Tagore's poem entitled "Anya Ma" in his collection of poems *Shishu Bholanath* in *Sanchayita*, 4th ed, 1943, p578-80

The first line of the original Bengali poem—
aamar maa na hoey tumi aar—kaaro maa holey

Published in POETRY WORLD, vol 4(no4), August 2011, pp16-18

55. GIFT

The day I bought you a pair of bangles
I thought it might please you.
You took them in your hand, turned them around
and looked at them for a moment,
May be you put them on when you went home
May be you then took them off and kept aside.
The night you came to say goodbye,
I noticed they were missing from your hands,
May be you just forgot, before you came.

The one who gives, what a state he gets into afterwards,
Why on earth does he even bother to remember the act!
The ripened fruit that drops onto the welcoming ground—
Does the branch of the tree cast an eye on it again?
The song that a bird tweets away in the air—
Does it ever try to remember it again?
In this world those who know how to give it away
They give their all in such a way that nothing is held back.

Those in turn, who know how to accept,
It is they, who know where the real value lies,
They only know that from the jewel-necklace
on one's bosom, how few can give away the gem
That a heart alone can see.
The one who happens to receive it, he gets it easily.
Receiving a gift that can be considered worth having,
Is not all that easy just because it is easily obtained—
One gets it only by providence.

When I begin to ponder, I can't find a clue—
what is there on earth that's worth giving anyway?

In which mine, in which treasury,
In bottom of—or across—the ocean
Or even in the necklace with countless jewels
Owned by the *Yaksha*—King,
There exists anything—my dear—that isn't but trivial.
That's why I say that whatever may be the gift I give,
It is by accepting it with all your heart,
You can make it precious.

Note:

Yaksha—King: the Hindu god of wealth.

English translation of Rabindranath Tagore's poem entitled "Daan" in his collection of poems *Purabi* in *Sanchayita*, 11ᵗʰ ed.2010, pp 604-5 .

The first line of the original Bengali poem—*kankan—jora ayne dilam jabey*

56. BONDAGE OF PATH

The path tied us in a knot
without attaching any string;
We both follow the direction
whichever way the wind blows.
Colourful moment—pampered by dust—
sprinkles red powder of *Holi* in life,
The monsoon clouds wave their veils
in dance performed by the courtesan of horizon—
When a flash of light suddenly strikes,
it coruscates our mind.

We don't have a golden *Champak* grove;
Neither have we a collection of *Bokul* trees
spread over the avenue.
Sometime in the evening, a nameless flower
suddenly spreads its smell,
In the morning—treating the sunshine with contempt—
Defiantly stands on top of the branches the bunch
of rhododendrons.

We don't have any savings of riches and wealth
nor were we brought up with tender loving care at home.
The bird on the roadside that wags its tail,
we don't put it in a cage—
We both are happy to hear it chirping
as it flies away relishing its freedom.
We incandesce with a rare glimmer of something
beyond comprehension that happens in a trice.

Note:

Holi: The Hindu spring festival of colour.

Champak: a flower or a tree of the Magnolia family.

Bokul; a large evergreen tree and its flowers

English translation of Rabindranath Tagore's poem entitled "Pather Bandhan" in his collection of poems *Mahua* in *Sanchayita*, 11ᵗʰed.2010, p625.

The first line of the original Bengali poem—*path bendhe dilo bandhan hin granthi* Published in POETRY WORLD vol.5(no2), June 2012, pp16-17.

57. FEARLESS

We are not going to make playthings of heaven on earth
being captivated by beautiful songs choked with tears.
We are not going to fill our bridal night with pleasantness
of the sting by five arrows of passion.
We will avoid begging with timid heart at the feet of destiny.
We have nothing to fear as we know for sure that we are
here to stay together both you and me.

We will fly high the banner of love while crossing inaccessible path
with unstoppable speed and performing uphill task.
Even if we have to face the misery of rough days,
we will still not call for truce nor ask for consolation.
If the oar breaks while crossing the river and the sail is torn apart,
faced with death we will know that where you are I am there too.,

We have seen the world through each other's eyes,
we have looked at each other too—
we both endured the heat of desert sand on path.
We never ran after any alluring mirage nor deceived ourselves
by turning truth into falsehood—
With this pride, we will carry on in this world as long as we live.
Let the message be glorified my love that you are here and
I am here too.

Note:
English translation of Rabindranath Tagore's poem entitled "Nirbhay"
in his collection of poems *Mahua* in *Sanchayita*, 11th ed. 2010, p627.

The first line of the original Bengali poem—
aamra dujana sarga-khelna garibo na dharanite

Published in The Visva—Bharati Quarterly Volume—22 Numbers 3 & 4
October—2013—March—2014 .p2.

58. EMPOWERED

Oh Lord, why wouldn't you give women the right
to determine their own destiny?
Bowing my head, why should I be waiting by the road-side
for fulfillment of some long awaited expectations
on an uncertain future date?
Should I just keep looking at the sky?
Why shouldn't I myself find my own road to success?
Why shouldn't I race my searching chariot
by firmly holding the reins of the powerful horses?
Brimming with supreme confidence, why can't I procure
the treasure of success from the inaccessible fortress
by staking my life if necessary.

I will not go to the bridal room
jingling anklets like a newly-wed—
Make me fearless with the spirit of love.
I will pick up the garland meant for the bride-groom
in my bold hands one day but has that auspicious time
quietly merged with the evening twilight?
I will never let him disregard my spirited resolve.
Meek submission will not command respect from him—
I will cast aside the cloak of my feeble shyness.

We will meet on the shore of the turbulent sea,
The passion of the roaring waves will carry
the triumphant sound of our meeting
onto the bosom of the horizon.
Removing the veil from my face I will tell him,
"In heaven and on earth, you are the only one for me."
At that moment the cry of the sea birds will be heard,
Following the western winds, they will feel
their way to the luminous Plough.

Don't leave me speechless my Lord—
The firebrand *Veena* is aroused in my blood.
After arriving at the peak moment of life,
let the very best words of life come streaming
through my voice in an uninterrupted flow.
What is beyond my capacity to express,
may my beloved access it by his heart.
If there is no more time left, then afterwards,
let that flowing stream quieten down
in the silence of the soundless ocean.

Note:
*veena:*a kind of musical string instrument.
English translation of Rabindranath Tagore's poem entitled"

The first line of the original Bengali poem—*naarike aapon bhagya joy koribar*

Published in The Visva-Bharati Quarterly Volume 23 Numbers 2&3
July—December 2014 pg1-2

59. JOURNEY

The King is going to war
amidst beating of drums and sounds of cymbals;
The whole earth is shaking.
The minister casts his net—of intrigues—wide
to pit one state against another so as to
tie them down in intricate knots.
The flow of commerce encircles the world
during the high and low tides alike.
Merchant ship rushes across
the shores of the sea.
The monument to commemorate glory
of the heroes is erected over the heap
of thousands of human skeletons—
Lifting its head high its summit looks
at the sky and roars with laughter.
The scholars repeatedly invade the impenetrable
castle of knowledge which is encircled by
the wall of books—
Their fame spreads widely from one country
to another.

Here near the outer limits of the village
the river flows slowly to the end of the
vast arid land with its current visibly decelerated.
The boat carrying the newly-wed bride
sails away to a distant village.
The sun sets and silence descends over the banks.
Palpitation grips the newly-wed's heart.
Slowly in the darkness, the evening star
becomes visible near the horizon.

Note:

English translation of Rabindranath Tagore's poem entitled "Yatra" in his collection of poems *Bichitra* in *Sanchayita*, 10ᵗʰ ed.2010, pp642-43.

The first line of the original Bengali poem—*raja kore ratha jatra baje bheri baje karatal*

Published in POETRY WORLD, vol. 6(no4), August 2013, pp 51-52.

60. A QUERY

Throughout the ages, Oh almighty God,
you have from time to time,
sent messengers to this merciless world—
They all said, "Forgive all—give love instead—
forsake all poison of malice from heart."
Revered they were, remembered they ought to be,
yet—facing a difficult time—I turned them away
from the gate with a token salute.

I have seen how covert violence under the cover of
treacherous night struck the hapless one,
I have seen—due to unchallenged crime committed
by the mighty—
how the voice of justice wept silently alone.
I also witnessed how a young boy running amuck,
banged his head against the stone in vain,
only to die in severe pain.

My voice is choked today; the flute has lost its tune,
The prison of new moon seems to have obliterated
my world under the cover of bad dreams.
That is why I ask you with tears in my eyes,
"Those who have poisoned your air and put out the lights,
did you ever pardon them, did you love them all?"

Note:
English translation of Rabindranath Tagore's poem entitled "Prashna" in his collection of poems *Parisesh* in *Sanchayita*, 11th ed.2010, pp645-6

The first line of the original Bengali poem—
bhagaban tumi juge juge dut pathayechha bare bare

Published in POETRY WORLD, vol 5(no1) April 2012, pp 13-14.

61. LETTER WRITING

You gave me a gold-plated fountain-pen
and all sorts of articles necessary for writing—
A small desk made of walnut-wood,
Printed letter-pads of many designs,
Silver paper—cut and enameled,
Scissors, knife, gum, red-ribbon,
A glass paper-weight
and also red, blue and green pencils.
Before going you said,
'Write you must every other day.'

I have just sat down to write the letter,
I already had bath in the morning.
I have no clue whatsoever what to write,
let alone the subject.
There is only one news and that is—
'You have gone away.'
But that's already known to you.
Still I feel that you do not comprehend it fully.
That is why; I think better I write and tell you
that you have gone away.
However, each time I start to write,
I realize it is not such simple news.
I am not a poet;
I am not able to give voice to the words
Neither can I exchange any glance with you.
Whatever I manage to write, I just tear it apart.

It is already 10 o'clock.
Your nephew Baku will be going to school,
Better I go and feed him first.
For the last time I write—
'You have gone away.'
Whatever else is there are only scribbles
and scrawls on the blotting paper.

Note:

English translation of Rabindranath Tagore's poem entitled "Patra lekha" in his collection of poems *Parisesh* in *Sanchayita*, 11ᵗʰ.ed.2010, pp646-47.

The first line of the original Bengali poem—*dile tumi sona moraa fountain pen*

62. IMMORTAL

From a distance I thought
You are invincible and ruthless;
The world trembles under your rule.
You are horror personified,
In the devastated heart of the afflicted one,
burns your blazing flame.
The missile in your right hand rising
towards the stormy sky
brings down the thunder from there.
Full of fear, I came in front of you
with a trembling heart.
Just the frowning of your eyes spelled imminent danger,
Then down came the strike.
My ribs quivered,
Pressing my chest with both hands I asked,
"Is there anything else left—
Is the thunder bolt still to come?"
Down came the strike.

This much only, there is nothing more?
Gone was my fright.
When your lightening was about to strike
I considered you to be bigger than me.
But with your strike you too came down
to the ground where I belong.
You have become small today
All my diffidence has disappeared..
However great you may be,
You are after all, not bigger than death.
'I am bigger than death,' saying these last few words
I will go away.

Note:

English translation of Rabindranath Tagore's poem entitled "Mrityunjoy" from his collection of poems *Parisesh* in *Sanchayita*, 11th.ed, 2010, p648.

The first line of the original Bengali poem—*dur hote bhebechhinu mone*

63. WATER-VESSEL

Oh God, you are the venerable one.
You the Lord of my life, you are fully aware
what caste I belong to.
Even then pushing aside everyone else on your way
Why—suffering what grief—you came in front of me!
Carrying the full pitcher on my waist,
following every turn on path in the field
—in intense heat in mid afternoon—
I was hurrying back home.
You asked me for water to quench your thirst—
I am a lowly woman-
That I will ignore you, would it be proper for me?
Putting the pitcher down and touching your feet
I said, "Please don't make me feel guilty."

Hearing this, you looked at my face with your
all conquering eyes,
Then you smiled and said, "Oh you daughter of the soil,
Where holy is the soil that makes this earth
—full of sweet dark complexion—
Likewise, you are the seat of Laxmi
and there you remain kissing her lotus feet.
The one who is beautiful has no caste,
she is always at liberty.
The sunlit dawn drapes her with its own clothes.
The star-studded night threads the bridal garland for her.
Please listen to me,
The hundred-petalled lotus has no particular caste.
The one who manifests the purest intention of heaven,
can she ever be untouchable?
When the Almighty Lord is satisfied with his own creation,
every day there is ablution with showering of blessings

from the whole world."
Saying this with a voice that resembles
the rumbling of a saturated cloud,
you went away.

From that time onwards
I paint this fragile pitcher of mine
—with the light of the dawn-in many a colour
and decorate its earthen cover by drawing many sketches.
Oh great Lord, for the one—for accepting whom—
You came down from your pedestal,
Let the offer of her beauty be carried forward to you

Note:

English translation of Rabindranath Tagore's poem entitled "Jalapatra" in his collection *Parishes* in *Sanchayita*, 11ᵗʰed, 2010, pp 652-54.

The first line of the original Bengali poem—*prabhu, tumi pujaniyo/aamar ki jaat*

64. A NEW COUNTRY

The boat is anchored in river near the *ghat*,
When I go to take a bath
I can see it dancing with the waves.

Today, when I went there and looked at a distance
I could see the boat in the middle of the river
going somewhere on the ebb-tide.

I do not know which country
it will eventually reach in the end,
What are the people there like
and how do they dress themselves!

I stay confined in the house,
I have a desire—oh brother—
that just like that I too can float along
to a new city with a new forest.

Far away along the coast of the sea near the water,
All the coconut groves are
standing tall in rows.

The peak of the mountain, adorns itself
in the middle of the sky,
Crossing over through the snow on top
is beyond the capacity of anyone.

I wonder in which forest and its undergrowth
—filled with new fruits and flowers—
so many new animals roam around in herds.

After so many nights, the boat is floating along—
Why does father bother to go to his office
and not go to a new country instead?

Note:

ghat: flight of steps leading to river landing place.

English translation of Rabindranath Tagore's poem entitled "Notun desh" from his collection of poems *Chitrabichitra* in *Sanchayita*, 11th.ed 2010, p758-59.

The first line of the original Bengali poem—*nadir ghaater kachhe nouko bandha aachhe*

65. CHITRAKUT

There was a small patch of land by the side of the kitchen,
It was the place where I used to play on the dried up grass.
There was a pile of ashes which looked like one big heap-
So much I tried and decorated it with the burnt out coals.
No one knew that it was a hillock what I imagined it to be,
Right at the bottom of that heap, I sowed a tamarind seed.
It was the birthday celebration of a six year old boy
And on that day, the first leaf appeared on my tree.
I surrounded it from all sides, with kerosene-tins
and watered it morning and evening day after day.
I regularly gave it a portion from my breakfast,
But most of it was eaten up stealthily by crows.
Some of my milk I gave without knowledge of others.
The ants used to drink some of it, the rest did the tree.
It got covered with tender leaves, the branches came out
Even before two years its height was same as that of mine.
That was my only tree, only a little was that corner—
That became my forest under the Mount *Chitrakut*.
No one knew that it was sage Astabakra who resided there—
His beard rolled on the ground and not one word he spoke.
Lying on bed at night, I could clearly hear the sounds—
The monsters would be hooting like owls at that place

My last play under that tree was on my ninth birthday—
I put a garland of flowers on its branches that morning.
Father left *Ranaghat* and he went to *Munsiganj*,
He put me under the care of my aunt at *Kolkata*.
When I lie on bed at night, I remember the tamarind tree
That grew up there in that corner of my rubbish dump.
Now there is no hermitage, heavenly river doesn't flow—
A long distance away has gone the sage Astabakra.

Note:

English translation of Rabindranath Tagore's poem entitled "Chitrakut" in his collection of poems *Chitrabichitra* in *Sanchayita,* 11th ed.2010, pp760-61

The first line of the original Bengali poem—*ektukhani jaigaa chhilo rannaghorer paashe*

66. ROYAL ORDER

The emperor—out of fear—stays put in the police station,
Whatever laws he promulgates, are never complied with.
His roving spies are always on the lookout and if by chance,
any saintly person strays and is found to be alone,
in that case they have to inform the king at once—
For his own safety, they keep the saint in prison.

Note:

English Translation of Rabindranath Tagore's poem entitled "Raj Byabastha" in his collection of poems *Chharar Chhabi* in *Sanchayita*, 4th ed.1943, p762

The first line of the original Bengali poem—*maharaja bhaye thake pulisher thanate*

Published in POETRY WORLD, vol 3(no9), January 2011, p29.

67. TIME FOR BIRD TO GO

It is time for the bird to depart
The abode will be empty soon.
With songs silenced, the detached nest
will drop down to the ground
-amidst stir of the forest
With the dry leaves and withered flowers
I will fly over an unchartered course
from this side of the sea at sunset on to
the other side at day break.

For such a long period this earth
has provided me with hospitality.
At times I received summons which
carried the smell of mango-blossoms
graced by the generosity of the
spring month of *Phalgun*.
The new leaves of the Ashoka tree
signaled to me to set the music which I lovingly did.
At times hit by the storm of the summer month of *Baisakh*
my voice got choked with hot sand and
my wings were immobilised.

All in all I am thankful for the honour
I received in life.
When this exhausting journey starting from
this side ends, I shall—for a moment—look back
and bowing my head with humility,
sing songs of praise of the presiding deity
of my birth.

Note:

*Phalgun:*the eleventh month of Bengali calendar, month of spring
*Baisakh :*first month of Bengali calendar
English translation of Rabindranath Tagore's poem entitled "Jaabar samay holo bihanger" in his collection of poems *Prankit* in *Sanchayita* 11thed, 2010 pp 775.

The first line of the original Bengali poem—*jaabar samay holo bihanger ekhani kulaya*

68. SAVING

You did not lend the touch of your right hand.
It is your light and shades that
-in the courtyard of imagination—draw and erase,
Besides painting off and on.

If the slender river of the month of *Baisakh*
failed to offer the grace of its full flow,
then it is the diffident shrunken stream that
aroused the thirsty mind on the side of its bank.

Whatever little of my muted desire
I could gather in my cupped palms
might not have over flown
but that's the saving at the end of the penury
of the whole day—
the collection of an entire lifetime dream.

Note:
English translation of Rabindranath Tagore's poem entitled 'Udbritta" in his
collection of poems *Saanai* in *Sanchayita*, 11th ed. 2010. p813.

The first line of the original Bengali poem—*taba dakkhin haater parash koroni samarpan*

Debidas Ray

69. RECEPTION

The blue colour of the mountain
and the blueness of the horizon
tune up words of prayer—
in sky and on earth.
The golden sunshine of the autumn
bathes the forest.
Amidst the bunch of yellow flowers,
the violet-hued bee searches for honey.
I happen to be there in the middle.
That is why the sky around me is clapping
without making noise.
In my moment of joy today,
sound and music have fused into one—
Does Kalimpong* know of this?

The mountain accumulates and stores
endless era and ages.
One special day of mine receives it
with a garland like a bride.
To convey this auspicious news—
far and further away in the sky—
in a tune not heard before,
the golden bell rings in the morning
making a resonating sound—
Is Kalimpong listening to this?

Note:
*Kalimpong, a picturesque hill station in Eastern Himalayas.
English translation of Rabindranath Tagore's poem entitled "Baran"
in his collection of poems *Janmadine* in *Sanchayita*, 11th ed.2010. p818.

The first line of the original Bengali poem—*paaharer nile aar diganeter nile*

Published in POETRY WORLD, vol.5(no.11), March 2013, p24.

70. HESITATION

In the land of Gods during dance festivals,
　　if even for a moment, a tired Urvashi
　　by chance misses a single step,
　　the King of Gods does not pardon her.

In venues where human beings meet
there too, the same rules of heavens apply.

That is why, there is diffidence underlying
　　my literary work because I fear that
　　　　due to exhaustion
　　at the end of a burning fevered day
there may occur—in such pursuit—laxity
　　and inadvertent faltering in steps.

Note:

English translation of Rabindranath Tagore's poem no.1 of *"Rogasajyay"* in Rabindra Rachanavali vol.3, p787.

The first line of the original Bengali poem—*surolokey nrityer utsabe*

Published in POETRY WORLD, vol 3(no 8), December 2010, p26.

71. DAY'S LAST SHADOW OF MINE

When the day's last shadow of mine
will merge with the basic melodious note
                              of the day—
its humming tone will linger for ever
though the exact meaning of it will be forgotten.

Tired with work, when the passer-by
                    will sit by the side of the road,
a faint trace of sadness of that tune
                         will touch his heart,
with head down, he will listen to it.

What he will get is only a mere hint and nothing more
other than this he will perceive that—
in days gone by—in a rare moment of history,
may be, there used to live someone who found
that something special which we all have been
                              searching for in vain.

Note:

English translation of Rabindranath Tagore's poem entitled "Aamaar diner shesh chhayatuku" in his collection of poems *Rogasajyay* in *Sanchayita*, 11th ed.2010, p819

The first line of the original Bengali poem—*aamar diner shesh chhayatuku*

Published in POETRY WORLD, vol.5(no8), December 2012, pp26-27.

72. TOY OF A LITTLE BOY

Khoka has lost his toy, his face is looking pale.
Mother said, 'Look, it's there hidden in the sky.'
Khoka asked, 'How did it disappear from the room?'
Mother said, 'It is those unruly boys from *Indralok*
Who just put it in a bag of clouds and took it away.'
Khoka said, 'When they came, when you came to know?'
Mother told, 'They came when you boys joined together;
Went into hiding in the mango forest of the Choudhuries
and damaged all of the fruits there without any qualms.
Overcast with clouds, the visibility was poor on that day
Their faces were covered with shadows from the trees.
None of us knew how many came and who they were.
Our dog too was fast asleep tucking his face under his tail.
Taking full advantage, stealthily they found out the room.
We thought the wind had struck the branches of bamboo trees,
Or maybe the squirrel ran across the roof of the thatched room.
At the time, overflowing the dam, water rushed out of the tank
Chanting *ho-ho*, the womenfolk gathered wanting to catch fish.
Blown by the storm, the top of palm-trees shook heads in air.
The window-shutters rattled at the sound of rumbling clouds.
I thought being a gentle boy, you were reading in your class.
I did not know when you had learnt all these naughty tricks.'

Khoka told, 'Oh Mother, all those children from *Indralok*,
Why did they get caught up in such nasty naughty pranks!
When they do manage to come and descend in the mango-forest,
They break the branches, pluck fruits and what a havoc they cause!
The fact is that the day the monsoon makes the whole forest swing,
What a chaos it creates between the branches, twigs and the leaves.
How can they really put their mind on their studies on such a day—
They go in a frenzy and holiday spree on banks of the Ajay River.
Afterwards, when things become quiet, they go back to their land-
Their mother scolds them and then tells them stories in the end.'

Debidas Ray

Note:

Khoka: little boy.

Indralok: abode of Indra the King of gods.

English translation of Rabindranath Tagore's poem entitled "Khokar khelna" from his collection of poems in *Galpasalpa* in *Sanchayita*, 11th ed, 2010, pp833-4.

The first line of the original Bengali poem—*khelna khokaar hariye gechhe*

104

73. PIYARI

Holding a lamp in hand, arrives in the courtyard,
the maiden daughter of the King, her name is Piyari.
When I asked her what she has come for,
she whispered to say, "I ask for nothing.
All I want is that you have a good look at me,
let the light of my lamp fill your mind in full.
Because I come and go across your door,
that's what makes the wind blow in *bakul* trees.
When the Jasmines bloom all over the forest,
I bring them in the expanse of my *sari* to show
them round.
Whatever flowers blossom anywhere in the forest,
they all get thrilled the moment I touch them.
When the morning star appears at dawn and you are alone,
it's me who goes and greets it properly.
As soon as my anklets start to tinkle,
the blades of the grasses start to shiver.
The flower-beds in your garden all dress themselves up
and whisper amongst themselves, 'Piyari has come.'
As the sun shines over morning clouds,
the forest wakes up to say, 'Piyari has come.'
When festival of spring arrives on *phalgun* full moon night,
there is tumult all round with cries of 'Piyari, Piyari.'
As the breeze revels in village amidst the mango blossoms,
the flutes everywhere start singing the tune of Piyari's name.
When water overflows in the Yamuna in autumn,
it keeps chanting, 'Piyari, Piyari,' across its banks."

Note:

*Bakul:*a large evergreen flower tree or its sweet scented flower.

*Phalgun:*the eleventh month of Bengali calendar (a month of spring)

English translation of Rabindranath Tagore's poem entitled "Piyari" in his collection of poems *Galpo salpo* in *Sanchayita*, 11ᵗʰ ed.2010, pp836-37.

The first line of the original Bengali poem—*aasilo dewari haate rajar jhiari*

Published in The Visva-Bharati Quarterly Volume 22 Numbers 3& 4 October-2013—March-2014 p3.

74. THE FIRST DAY'S SUN

Upon arrival of the new entity,
the sun of the first day
asked the question,
"Who are you?"
There was no answer.

After many years elapsed,
the day's last sun
at the western shore of the sea
-in quietness of the evening-
asked for the last time,
"Who are you?"
Didn't get any reply.

Note:
English translation of Rabindranath Tagore's poem entitled "Pratham Diner Surya" in his collection of poems *Shesh Lekha* in*Sanchayita*, 11th ed.2010, p838.

The first line of the original Bengali poem—*pratham diner surya*

Published in POETRY WORLD, vol.5 (no1)April, 2012 p.14.

75. THE PATH TO YOUR CREATION

The path that leads to your creation
-Oh illusive Mother-
you have bestrewed it with amazing webs of deception.
With deft hand, you have entrapped our simple life
in an intrigue of false notions.
By this deceitful method, you have tainted what
was sublime,
you did not even spare it the reclusiveness
of the night.
The path that your stars lead one onto
is the way to his heart which is always transparent,
Relying on good faith, he keeps it illuminated forever.
He may outwardly be deceptive but he is straight within
and that is his pride.
Though people consider him to be deprived,
he is the one who finds the truth which is flooded
with light of his inner self.
Nothing can ever deceive him.
It is he who carries home the ultimate award.
The one who has the capacity to face deceptions
with ease
is the one who gets from you the right over
everlasting peace.

Note:

English translation of Rabindranath Tagore's poem entitled "Tomar Shristir Path" in his collection of poems *Shesh Lekha* in *Sanchayita,* 11th ed.2010, p839.

The first line of the original Bengali poem—*tomar sristir path rekhechho akirno kori*

Pubished in POETRY WORLD, vol.5(no4), August 2012, p42.

BIOGRAPHY

A Medical Practitioner by profession and indulging in literary writings in between as a hobby, Dr Debidas Ray was born in Bishnupur of Bankura District in West Bengal in India. He did his schooling and spent his childhood there. He used to write Bengali poems which were published in school and local magazines. He studied Intermediate Science at Ramakrishna Mission Vidyamandir at Belur Math and undergraduate Medicine at Kolkata. He did his post graduate studies In UK where he spent a decade and worked in several hospitals.

Returning to India he joined the Maulana Azad Medical College at Delhi and thereafter worked in the Christian Medical College, Vellore until retirement. For the next five years as an Emeritus Medical Scientist of the Indian Council of Medical Research, he carried out research projects at Chennai. Throughout his professional career though very busy in patient care, teaching and research, his writing habit remained with him. He wrote scores of scientific papers in Medicine which were published in well known Journals in India and abroad.

It is after retirement and abatement of routine work when his earlier literary habit returned and he again started writing Bengali poems and a book of the poems was published. Over the last decade, he has been writing English poems which have been published in reputed English Journals throughout India. For the last five years he has been extensively translating Tagore's original Bengali poems into English which are being published in prestigious journals including the Visva Bharati Quarterly founded by Rabindranath Tagore.

Currently he resides with his wife at Vellore and runs a Chest Clinic at Sathuvachari. He is an active member of many professional bodies, literary organizations and cultural societies. He is an avid reader and regularly writes articles and poems for journals, magazines and anthologies.